Even a Stone Buddha Can Talk

Even a Stone Buddha Can Talk

The Wit and Wisdom of Japanese Proverbs
Volume 2

Compiled and translated by
DAVID GALEF

Illustrations by
JUN HASHIMOTO

Tuttle Publishing
Boston · Rutland, Vermont · Tokyo

First published in 2000 by Tuttle Publishing, an imprint of Periplus Editions (HK) Ltd, with editorial offices at 153 Milk Street, Boston, Massachusetts 02109.

Library of Congress Cataloging-in-Publication Data

Even a stone Buddha can talk : more wit and wisdom of Japanese proverbs / compiled and translated by David Galef ; illustrations by Jun Hashimoto.--1st ed.
    p. cm.
  English and Japanese.
  ISBN 0-8048-2127-5 (pbk.)
  1. Proverbs, Japanese--Translations into English. 2. Proverbs, Japanese. 3. Proverbs, English. I. Galef, David. II. Hashimoto, Jun.
PN6519.J3 E93 2000
398.9'956--dc21   99-059438

Distributed by

USA
Tuttle Publishing
Distribution Center
Airport Industrial Park
364 Innovation Drive
North Clarendon, VT 05759-9436
Tel: (802) 773-8930
Tel: (800) 526-2778

JAPAN
Tuttle Shuppan
RK Building, 2nd Floor
2-13-10 Shimo-Meguro, Meguro-Ku
Tokyo 153 0064
Tel: (03) 5437-0171
Fax: (03) 5437-0755

CANADA
Raincoast Books
8680 Cambie Street
Vancouver, British Columbia
V6P 6M9
Tel: (604) 323-7100
Fax: (604) 323-2600

SOUTHEAST ASIA
Berkeley Books Pte Ltd
5 Little Road #08-01
Singapore 536983
Tel: (65) 280-1330
Fax: (65) 280-6290

First edition
06 05 04 03 02 01 00   10 9 8 7 6 5 4 3 2 1

Design by Christopher Kuntze

Printed in United States of America

Contents

Foreword

Proverbs are short pithy sayings that embody general truths. As such, they provoke us to consider the extent to which truth exists at all. Some of the proverbs here are straightforward; others are more rhetorically complex. Take the Japanese saying "The ocean does not choose its trash" (number 11), for instance. It has great resonance these days, since the degradation of our natural environment weighs more and more heavily upon our minds. Yet this fact about oceans is not the real point of the saying at all. This proverb uses this truth in a metaphorical way to establish another, less evident one. Like our oceans, which are utterly receptive to anything that wind and water bring to them, a generous soul is open to all those around him. By way of one truth, we reach another. But is the second truth really true?

Perhaps this masquerade is needed because "The ocean does not choose its trash" is an injunction. Perhaps we naturally resist the type of wisdom that asks us to wise up. Other proverbs are less moralizing and, therefore, rhetorically more simple. Consider, for instance, "Water in a sleeping ear" (number 14). This saying does little more than describe a moment of total surprise. The Japanese say *"Nemimi ni mizu"* frequently in the sense that something is news to them. There is no inducement to action of any kind. The "general truth" of water in a sleeping ear seems to lie much more in the surprise of being suddenly wakened from a nap than in any kind of ideation that might follow. There is no second truth. "A carp on a cutting board" (33), a proverb that expresses total helplessness, is similar in this way.

What is true about either of these two different types of proverbs—those that incite and moralize and those that simply describe a situation—is that both are visually powerful. Both create an image that lingers in the mind by establishing a cognitive hook on which to hang on idea or two. Often the images are arresting— "To chew sand" (34) or "A fire from a kimono sleeve" (71). Their vividness forces us to entertain the truth in its particular situation and to remember its connection with experience. In other words, without seeing truth in a lived context, we come up empty. A *kotowaza* (or proverb) is meaningless unless we can do this. If there is no imagination, there is no truth.

This tendency to make meaning visual (and lyrical) is a fundamental feature of Japanese aesthetics. The propensity explains why, for instance, the brief lyricism of a thirty-one-syllable *waka* or a seventeen-syllable *haiku* can justify interpretation after interpretation, meaning after meaning, translation after translation, when they are often nothing more than a statement of observation. Here is just one famous example, loosely translated from Matsuo Bashō's *Journey to the Deep North*:

> In the silence of the temple,
> a cicada's voice
> penetrates the rocks.

The proverbs contained in *Even a Stone Buddha Can Talk* share such brevity. Because of this, they similarly thirst for the visible context of their truth.

For the translator, brevity and its call for the situational nature of proverbial truth poses considerable problems. In David Galef's preface to the previous volume, *Even Monkeys Fall from Trees* (1987), he explains the rather complicated process that led to the features of that enjoyable book (which are repeated in this second volume). First, we start with a Japanese original; then comes a fairly literal translation of the proverb; then a Western equivalent of the same; and, finally, a graphic translation. ". . . I felt continually that something was missing," he writes. "In attempting to describe the meaning of *Uma no mimi ni nenbutsu* (A sutra in a horse's ear), I realized what it was I wanted: a slightly bored horse, perhaps wearing a sun-hat, being lectured to by a patient priest—in a word, illustration."

Jun Hashimoto has collaborated with Galef once again to make another one hundred Japanese proverbs come to life. They make a good pair. Whether word or figure, their work is true to the situational, experiential emphasis of Japanese aesthetics in general, and of proverbial wisdom in particular. Just as, say, the brief poems of *The Tale of Ise* require prose explanations of the particular moment that led to the creation of a particular poem, so, too, do Hashimoto's images make us consider the particular moment of the proverb, the truth of real life that generates wisdom.

Our attempt to imagine an actual moment of truth is, of course, the very pleasure of this book and, beyond this, a reason to applaud the continuing life of conventional wisdom. For no other form of writing makes us more curious about its provenance than the proverb. Who was it, for instance, who first stated the devastating truth, "You can't smell your own bad breath" (69)? Or what bad experience led someone to utter for the first time, "Blowfish is tasty, but life is precious" (51)?

Certainly, neither bad breath nor death by blowfish happened just once. We assume a repeatability of experience, freed from the linearity of modern history and able to jump handily over cultural borders, though there are exceptions, such as "Swimming on a tatami mat" (24). In other words, one attractive quality of these pithy sayings is precisely the difficulty we would have in trying to imagine a single moment of their creation. To the extent that such a moment both escapes us and seems totally imaginable, the proverbs take on an aura of universality and even timelessness.

The same cannot be said for the slogan and the tag line, which dictate experience rather than are dictated by it. With these, we can easily imagine a single person, or perhaps a committee, concocting a verbal formula. In Japan, the slogan reigned during the Meiji period (1868–1912), with "Civilization and Enlightenment" (*Bunmei kaika*), "Rich Country, Strong Army" (*Fukoku kyōhei*), "Personal Success at All Costs" (*Risshin shusse*), and so on. But these do not express wisdom. Wisdom has no agenda. It is no one's servant but everyone's teacher. That is why, as Galef shows us, rough equivalents exist in other cultures. To the extent that this is true (and sometimes there just isn't a perfect fit), the same must be said of truth. It belongs to no one, while we all belong to it. Any other kind of truth is just someone's opinion.

Charles Shiro Inouye
Tufts University

Preface

If sequels sometimes suffer by comparison to the original works, the same applies to their prefaces. Of course, this problem may be merely a matter of perception, a sense of belatedness or the difficulty of following a good act. If the first work was good, anything less than better seems second-rate. We still consider ourselves lucky that our first collection of proverbs, *Even Monkeys Fall from Trees*, turned out to be so popular.

In the first book, we explored the realm of Japanese folk wisdom, at times startlingly like the accumulated lore of the West, at other times presenting a completely different face in the mirror (or window—so much depends on the metaphor, as in proverbs). *Shikaku na zashiki o maruku haku*, for example, "to sweep a four-cornered room in a circle," translates easily into the proverbial phrase "to cut corners." On the other hand, *Rei mo sugireba burei ni naru*, "Exceeding courtesy becomes rudeness," seems quintessentially Japan-

ese, as anyone can attest who's seen two arguers retreat
into ever-icier polite forms of address. "Killing with
kindness," though it shares the same spirit, seems a
trifle lame as an equivalent.

These kinds of perplexities have attracted a lot of
readers. In fact, over a decade since its first printing, our
first proverbs book is still used in language and culture
classes. So we decided to do it again—but this time, ex-
plore some of the deeper realms of Japanese proverbial
wisdom. *Kireba kizamushi*, for instance, "The more
you wear, the colder you feel," may not make much
sense to a Western readership, but its nugget of truth,
something like "The greedy are never satisfied," should
be resonant everywhere.

As always with these kinds of projects, the act of
translation (and the task for readers) involves a double
projection: first, to throw oneself into the world of
another culture, and second, to travel back centuries to
when life was often a short, hard scrabble in the soil, and
existence itself depended on the sometimes-grudging
cooperation of neighbors. The saying *Shinda ko no toshi
o kazoeru*, "counting a dead child's years," is simply
heartbreaking. But in the days of high infant-mortality,
it was a rather common occurrence and aptly describes
a fruitless endeavor. In any event, one needn't agree
with Thomas Hobbes's famous sum-up of life, "solitary,
poor, nasty, brutish, and short"—not when there are
apothegms like *Nasake ni hamukau yaiba nashi*, "No
sword can oppose kindness." Nor do images of samurai
and antique weaponry restrict the usage to olden days.
Anyone who surveys how societies change will recog-

nize that pettiness and generosity merely find new outlets.

Still, each proverb carries a miniature history in its phrasing, and the translator's job is to render a close approximation of the original. Extra flourishes, such as changing the verb or even the image, is not only a different kind of translation, but should be rendered unnecessary by the explanatory illustrations and the Western equivalents listed in the index. If the Western reader doesn't understand what "*Hyōtan de namazu o osaeru*" means ("to pin down a catfish with a gourd"), study the accompanying picture. If that doesn't help, a quick perusal of the index will show "slippery as an eel," which renders the sense if not quite the same flavor. The taste of these phrases varies from crude to refined, the feeling behind them big-hearted but just as often cruel. These are concentrated chunks of wisdom, hard-won from experience, so perhaps *practical* is the best-fitting term.

If you want to learn more, read the book. After all, *Gakumon ni chikamichi nashi*: "There is no shortcut to scholarship." (Friends and family help, however, and in the making of this collection, we'd like to acknowledge particularly the help of Beth Weinhouse and Michiko Hashimoto.)

David Galef
University of Mississippi

The Proverbs

日本の諺

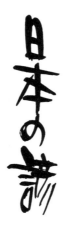

1

Ishibotoke mo mono o iu.

Even a stone Buddha can talk.

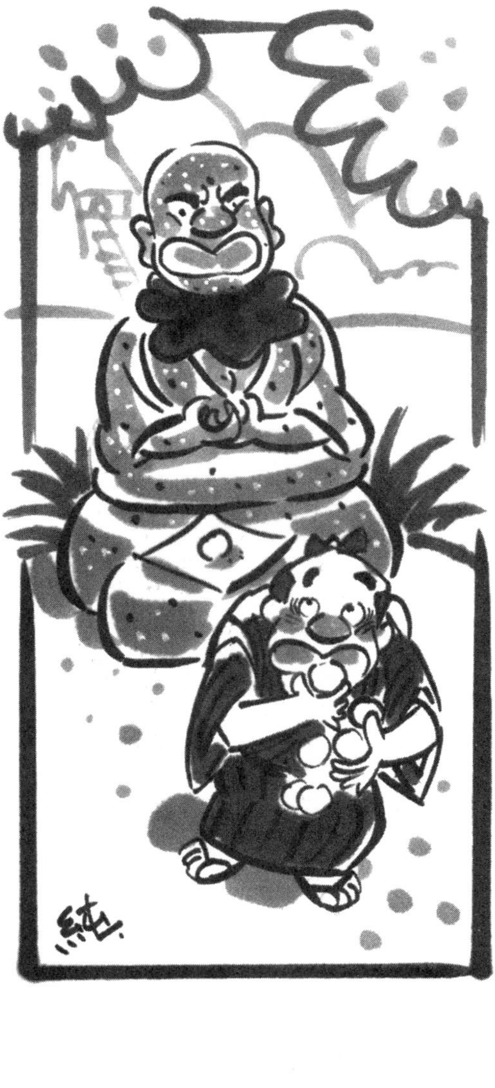

石仏も物を言う

2

Shishi shinchū no mushi.

Worms in the middle of a lion's body.

獅子奉中の虫

3

Tesha yori nasha ga kowai.

A person with nothing is more fearsome than one with talent.

有着より　無着が怖い

4

Tsuki yuki hana wa ichido ni nagamerarenu.

The moon, snow, and flowers cannot all be viewed at the same time.

月雪花は一度に眺められぬ

5

Nagakōjō wa akubi no tane.

A long speech is the source of yawns.

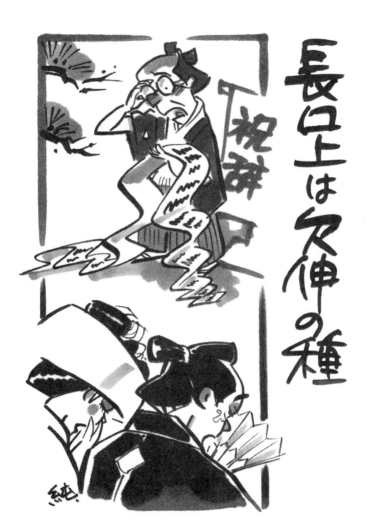

長口上は欠伸の種

祝詞

6

Muyō no yō.

A use for the useless.

無角の角

7

Shindai ni tsururu-kokoro.

Hanging one's heart on wealth.

身代につるる心

8

Shindako no toshi o kazoeru.

Counting a dead child's years.

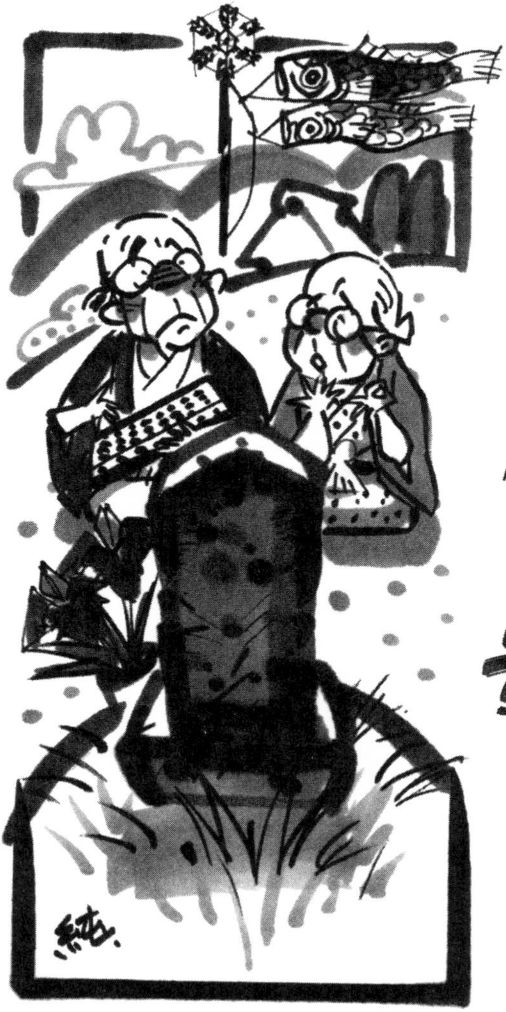
純

死んだ子の年を数える

9

Neko ni koban.

A gold coin to a cat.

猫 K 小判

10

Rei mo sugireba burei ni naru.

Exceeding courtesy becomes rudeness.

礼も過ぎれば　無礼になる

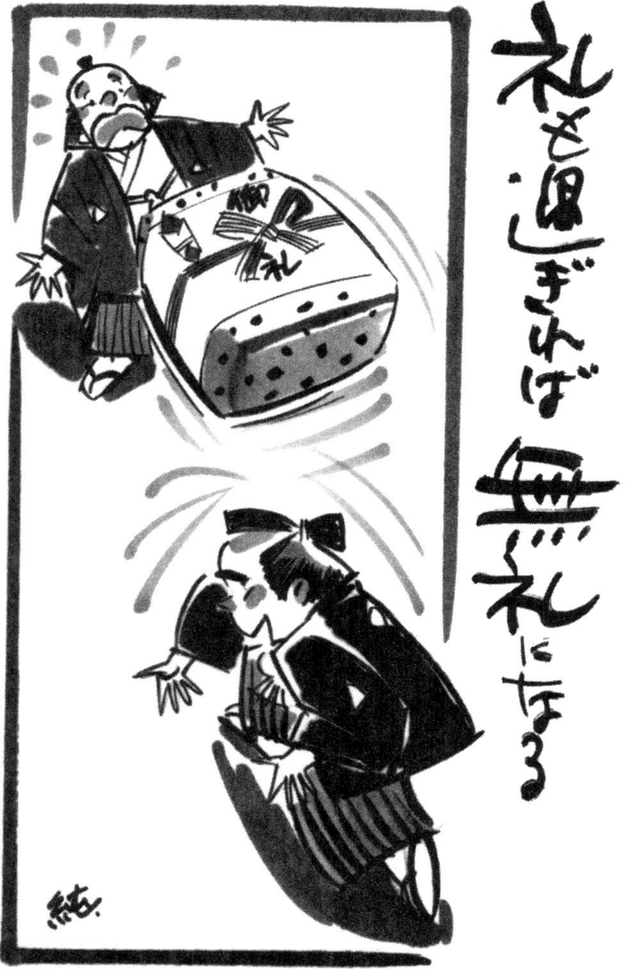
御礼

11

Taikai wa akuta o erabazu.

The ocean does not choose its trash.

大海は芥を択ばず

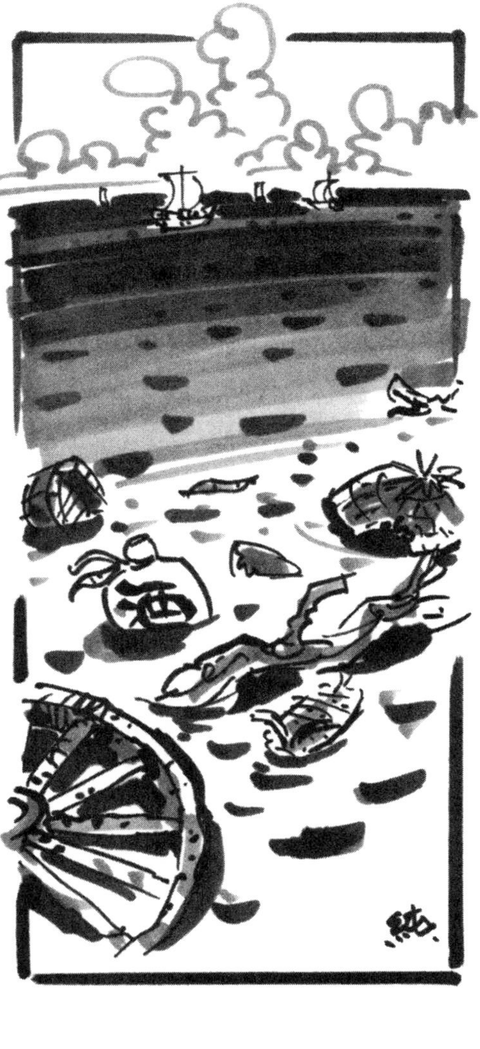
酒

12

Taiki bansei.

Genius matures late.

大業晩成

13

Yoki funbetsu wa setchin de deru.

Wise judgment comes when on the toilet.

善き人の別は雷隠で出る

14

Nemimi ni mizu.

Water in a sleeping ear.

寝耳に水

15

Shini uma ni hari o sasu.

To stick needles in a dead horse.

死に馬に、鍼をさす

16

Heso de cha o wakasu.

To boil tea on one's navel.

臍で茶を沸かす

17

Nikumarekko yo ni habakaru.

The hateful child does as he pleases in the world.

憎まれっ子世にはばかる

18

Ruri mo hari mo teraseba hikaru.

Emeralds and crystals glitter when lit.

瑠璃と玻璃と照らせば光る

19

Nodomoto sugireba atsusa o wasureru.

Once past the throat, hot liquid is forgotten.

喉元過ぎれば熱さを忘れる

20

Kiite gokuraku mite jigoku.

Hearing heaven, seeing hell.

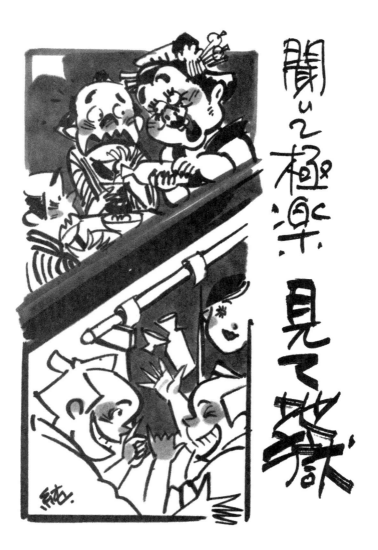

聞いて極楽　見て地獄

21

Raku wa ku no tane, ku wa raku no tane.

Pleasure is the source of pain; pain is the source of pleasure.

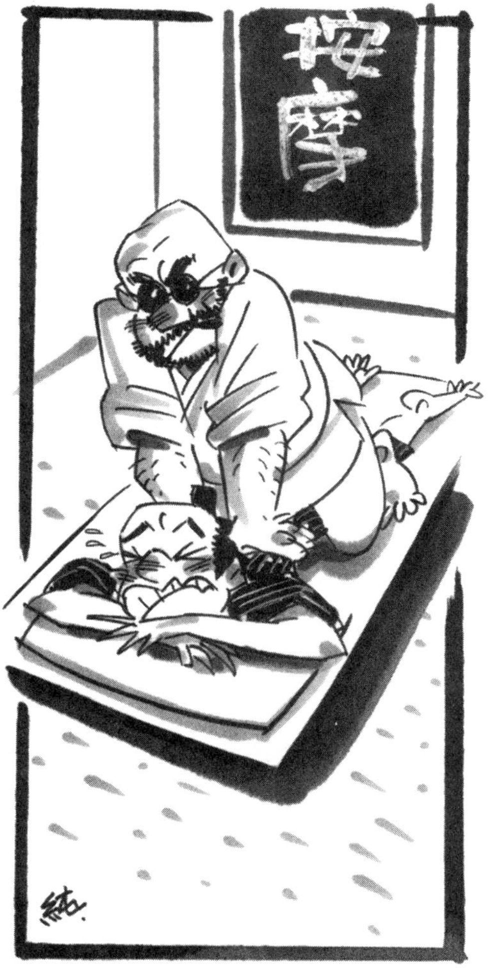
按摩

楽は苦の種、苦は楽の種

22

Korobanu saki no tsue.

A cane before falling.

転ばぬ先の杖

23

Tada yori takai mono wa nai.

There is nothing more costly than what's free.

ただより高いものはない

24

Tatami no ue no suiren.

Training to swim on the tatami.

畳の上の水練

25

Shikaku na zashiki o maruku haku.

To sweep a four-cornered room in a circle.

四角な座敷を丸く掃く

26

Shoku gataki.

Work-enemies.

職がたき

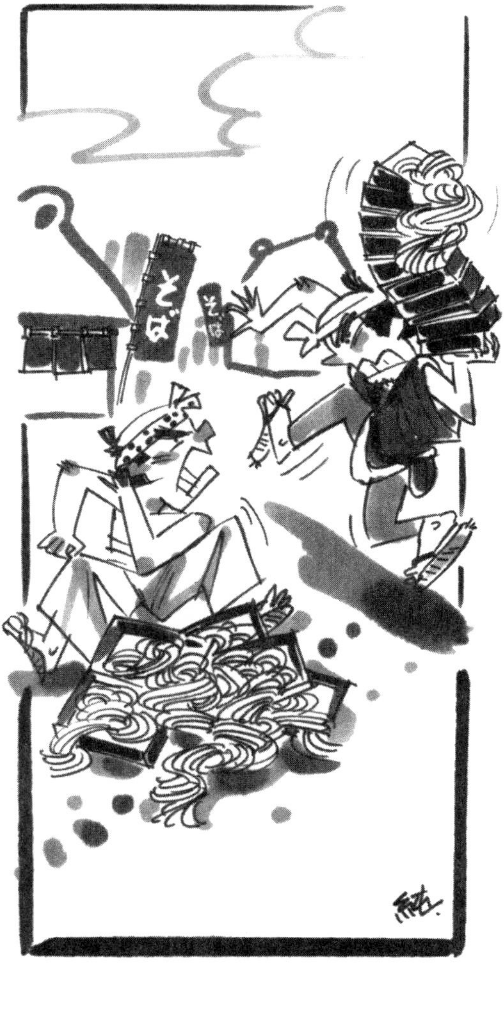
そば
そば

27

Me wa kuchi hodo ni mono o iu.

The eyes speak as well as the mouth.

目は口程に物を言う

28

Nusubito to chisha no sō wa onaji.

Thieves and scholars look the same.

盗人と智者の相は同じ

29

Tsuki-yo ni kome no meshi.

A meal of rice under the evening moon.

月夜に米の飯

30

Suigyo no majiwari.

The mingling of water and fish.

水魚の交わり

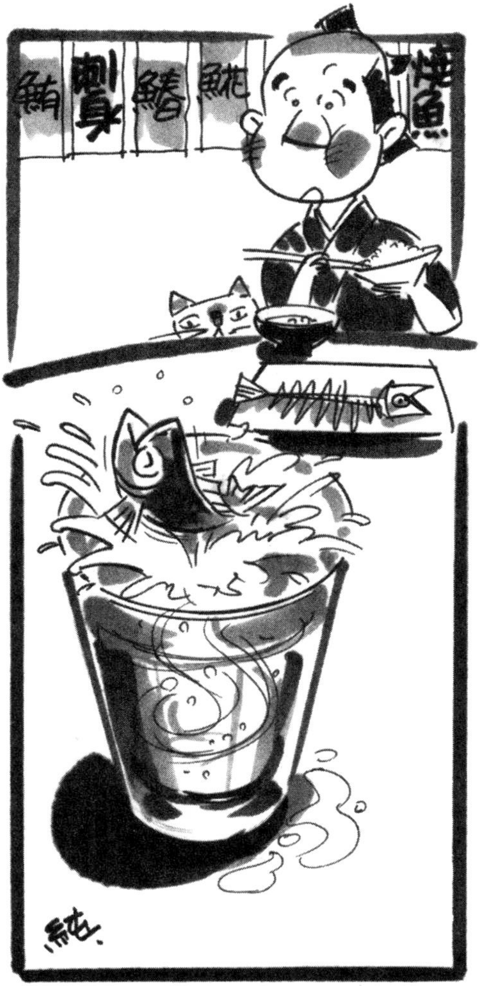

鮪
刺身
焼魚

31

Kōryō kui ari.

An exalted dragon suffers hardship.

亢龍悔い有り

32

Nusumi-gui wa umai.

Stolen food is tasty.

盗み食いはうまい

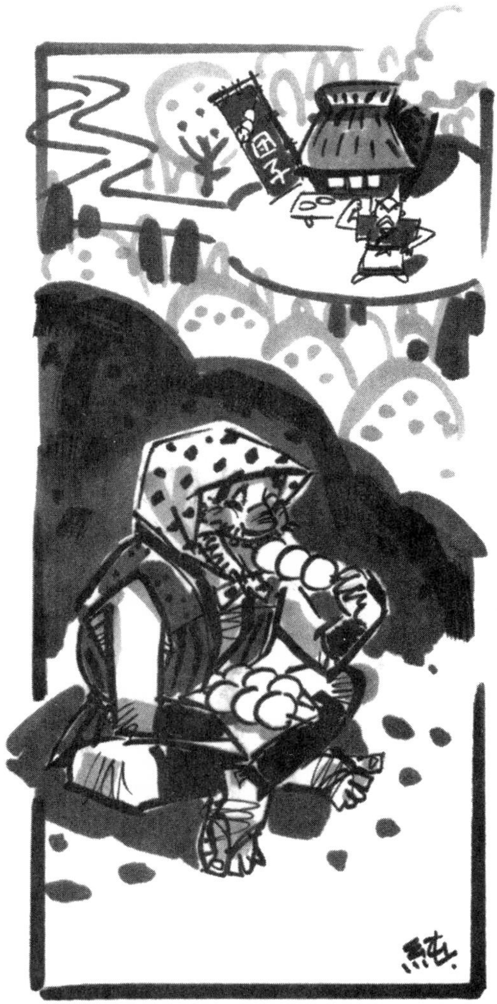
団子

33

Manaita no koi.

A carp on a cutting board.

俎板の鯉

日本の諺

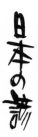

34

Suna o kamu.

To chew sand.

砂と勝男

35

Nasake ni hamukau yaiba nashi.

No sword can oppose kindness.

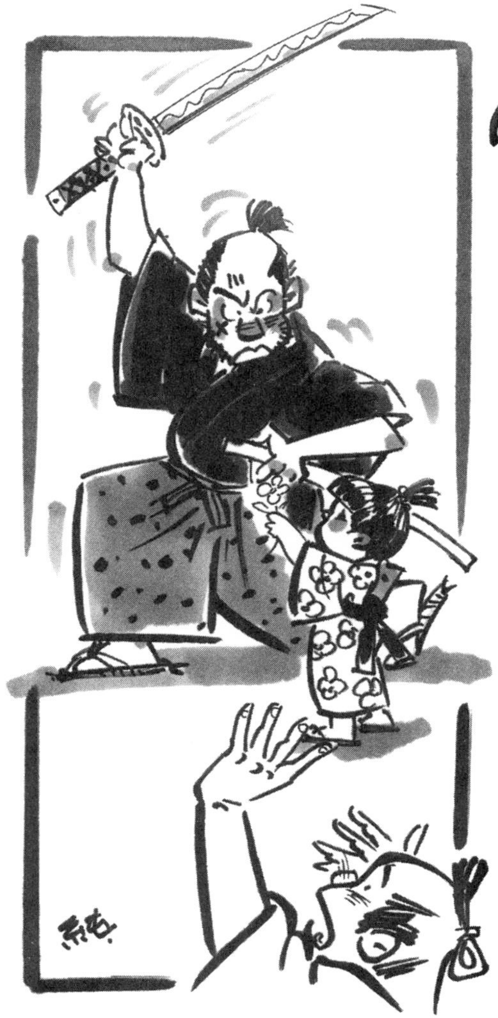

情けん刃回っ刃なし

36

Ichijō no ya wa orubeku,
jūjō wa orubekarazu.

One arrow can easily break;
ten arrows do not easily break.

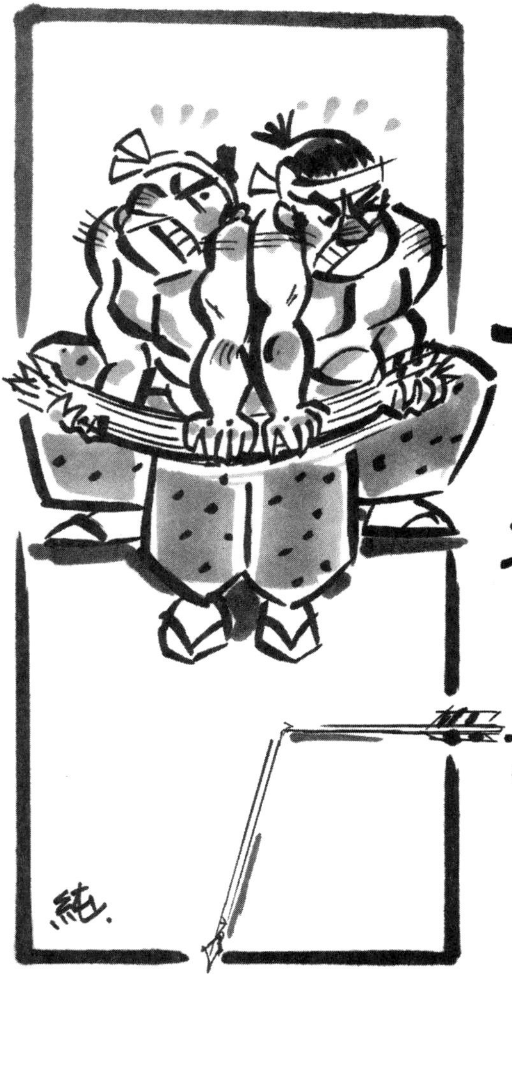

一条の矢は折べく
十条は折べからず

37

Hanashi-jozu no kiki-beta.

Good at talking, bad at listening.

話し上手の聞き下手

38

Boro o kite mo kokoro wa nishiki.

Though he wears rags, his heart is brocade.

襤褸を着ても心は錦

39

Zen naru mono kanarazu bi narazu.

What becomes good does not necessarily become beautiful.

善なるその必ず美ならず

40

U no mane o suru karasu, mizu ni oboreru.

A crow imitating a cormorant drowns in the water.

鵜の真似をする烏　水に溺れる

41

Hayaku jukusureba hayaku kusaru.

If it ripens quickly, it rots quickly.

早く熟すれば　早く腐る

42

Mekura hebi ni ojizu.

The blind do not fear snakes.

盲蛇に怖じず

43

Gakumon ni chikamichi nashi.

There is no shortcut to scholarship.

学問に近道なし

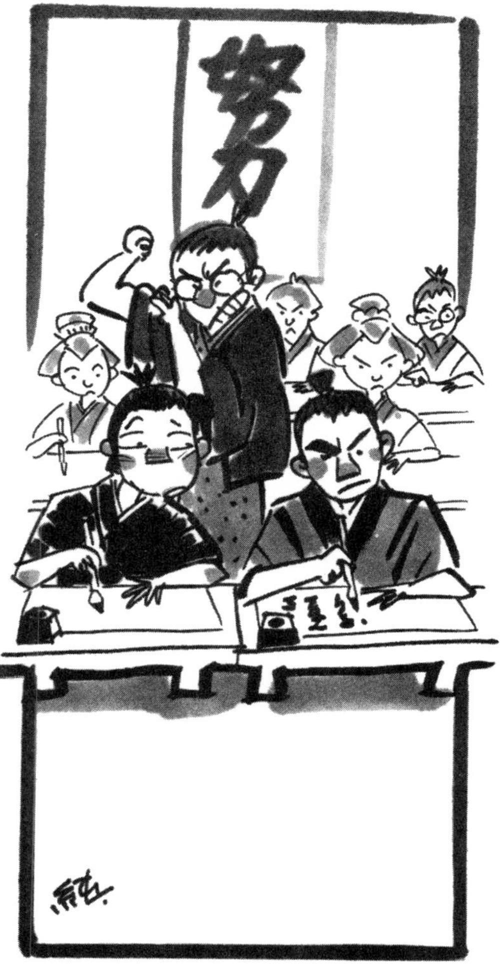
努力

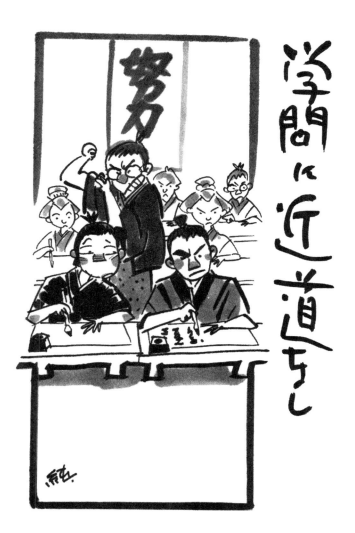

44

Teki ni shio o okuru.

Send salt to your enemy.

敵に塩を贈る

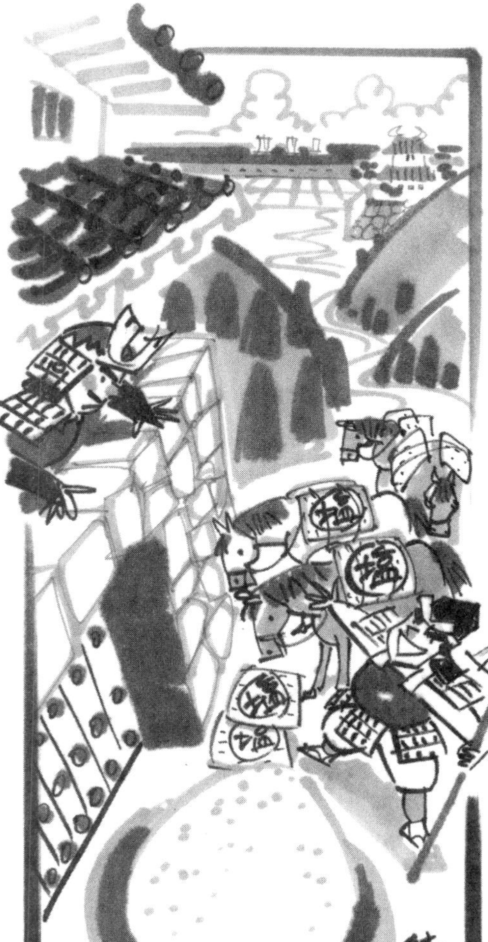
塩
塩
塩
塩
純

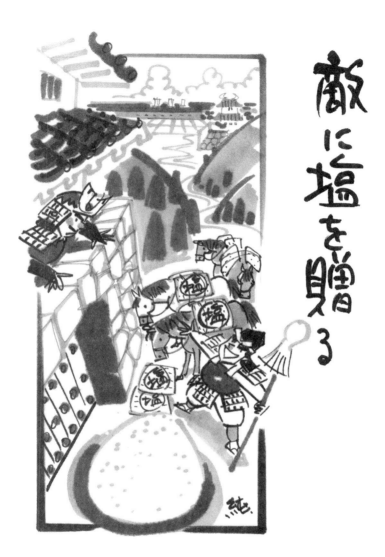

45

Aru ichi mon nai sen ryō.

To have one mon is better than not to have a thousand ryō.

有る一文、無い千両

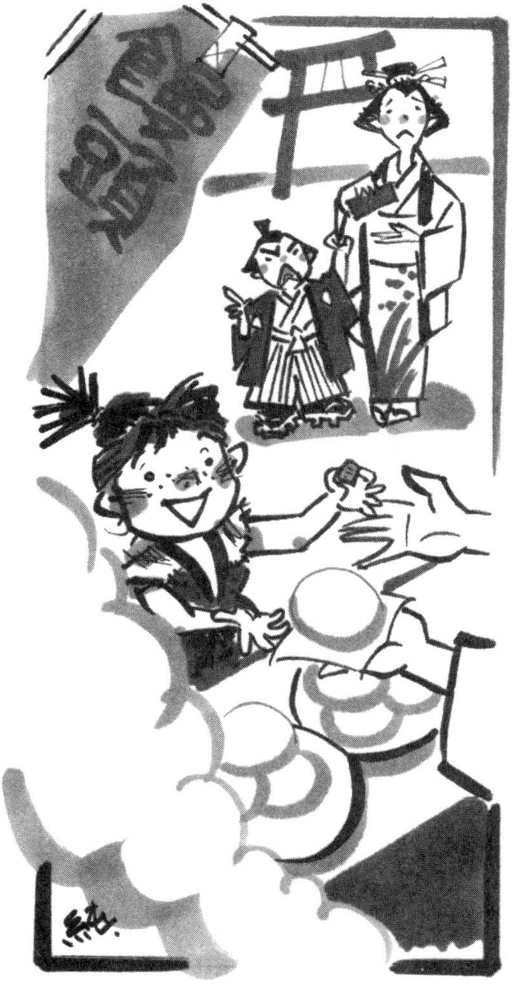
饅頭

46

Go ni katte shōbu ni makeru.

Winning at go, losing the competition.

碁に勝って勝負に頂ける

47

Kireba kizamushi.

The more you wear, the colder you feel.

着ぶくれば 着寒さ

48

Shizoku no shōhō.

A warrior's business practices.

士族の商法

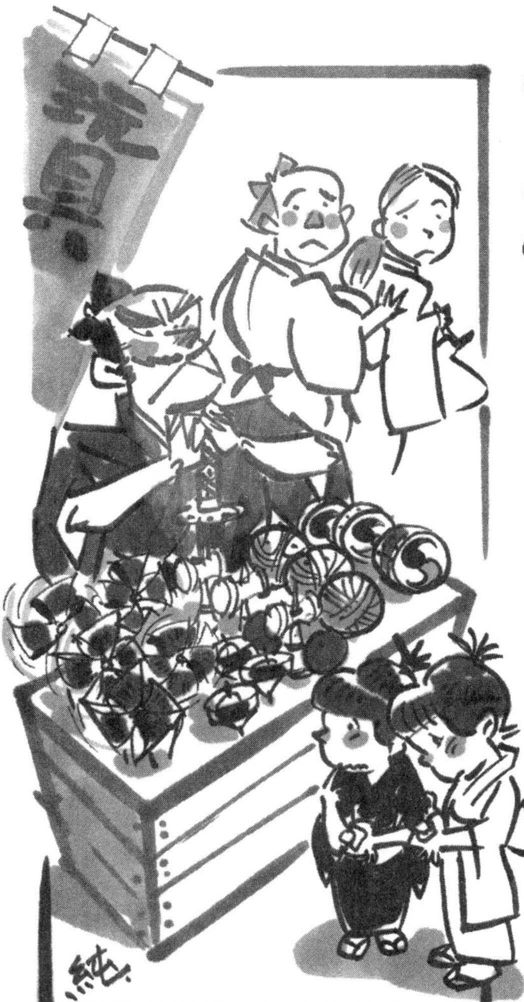

49

Tōdai moto kurashi.

Darkness at the base of the lighthouse.

燈台下暗し

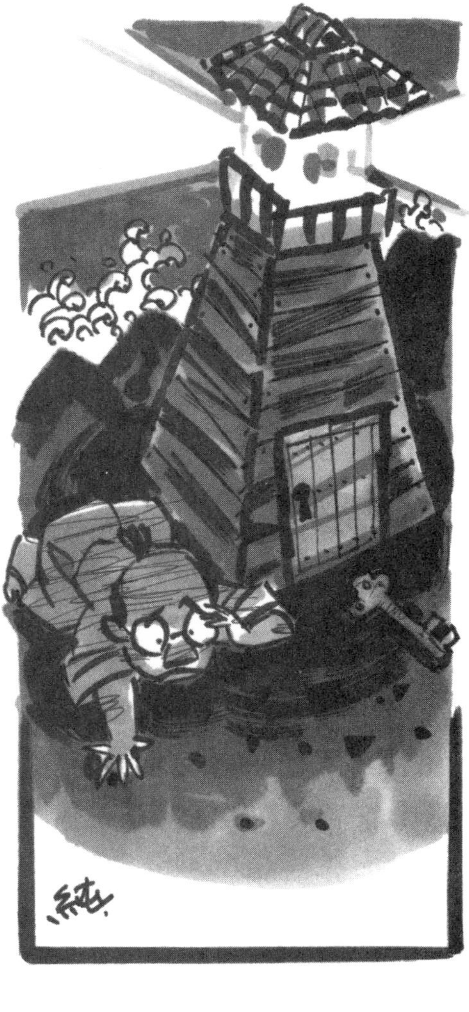
純

50

Endō wa hikage de mo hajikeru.

Beans grow even in the shade.

豌豆は日陰でそはじける

51

Fugu wa kuitashi inochi wa oshishi.

Blowfish is tasty, but life is precious.

河豚は食いたし命は惜しし

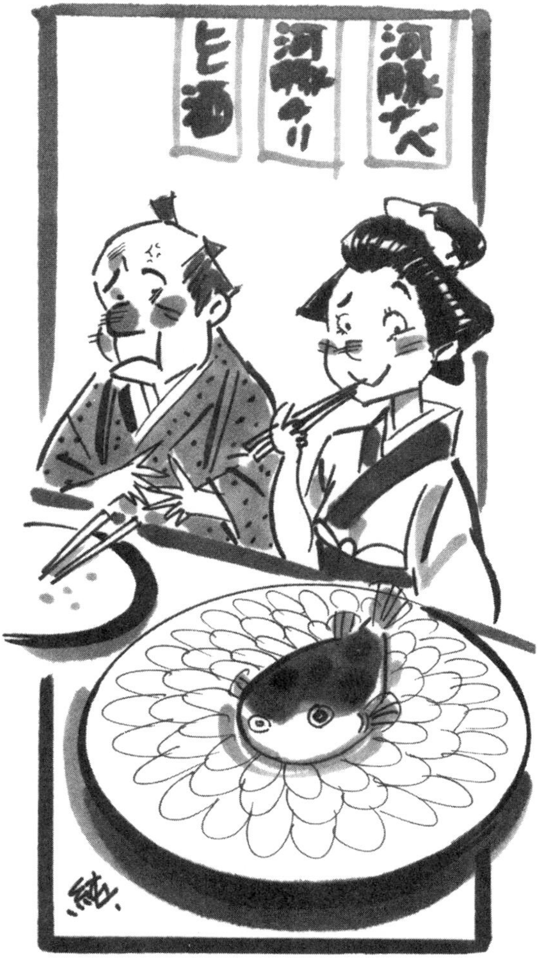
河豚なべ
河豚チリ
ヒレ酒
純

52

Haigun no shō wa hei o katarazu.

A defeated army's general should not talk about tactics.

敗軍の将は兵を語らず

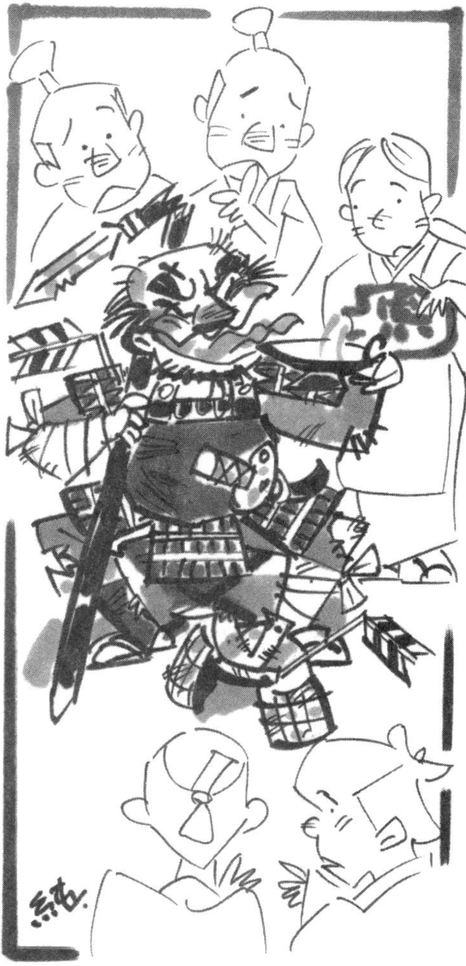

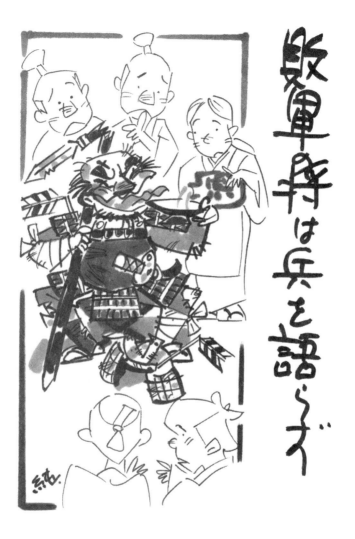

53

Kakusu koto wa kuchi yori dasuna.

Do not let secrets leave your mouth.

隠すことは 口ょぃ出すな

54

Kyo wa ki o utsusu.

One's residence affects one's mood.

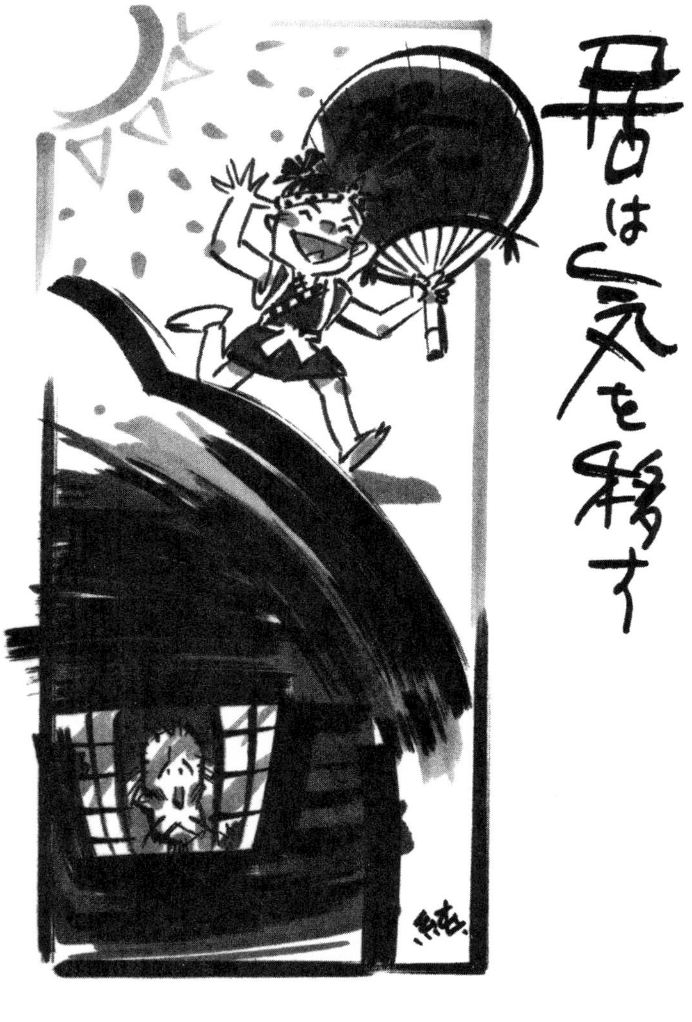
居は気を移す

55

Mukashi wa ima no kagami.

The past is the mirror of today.

昔は今の鏡

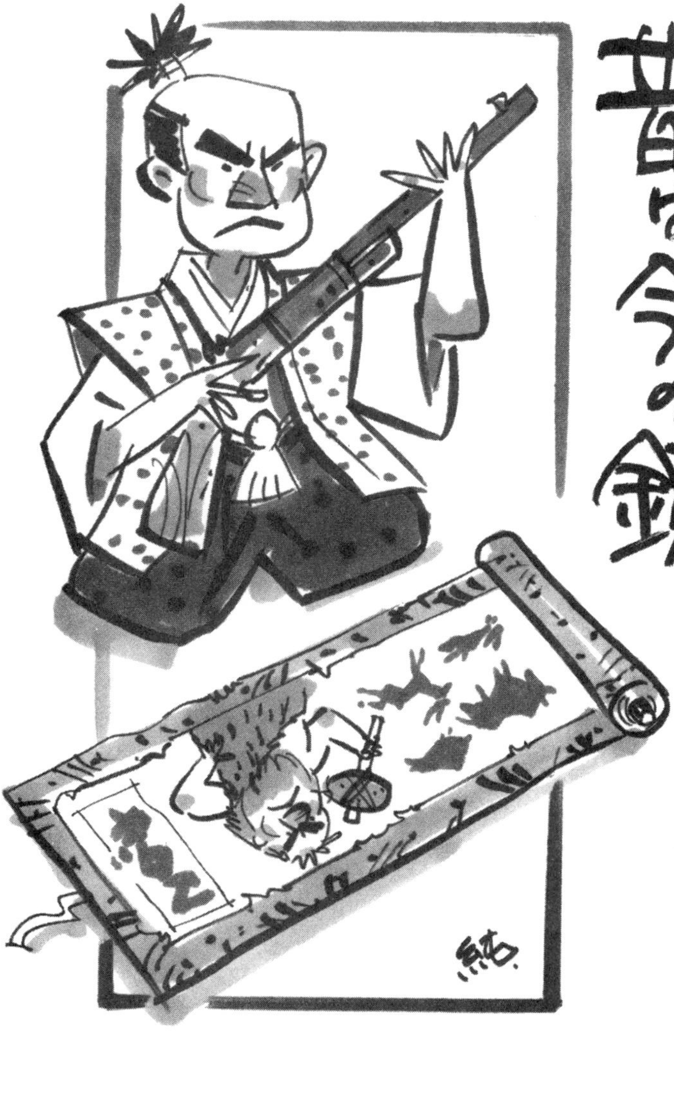

56

Ki ni mochi ga naru.

Rice cakes grow on trees.

木ぃ餅がなる

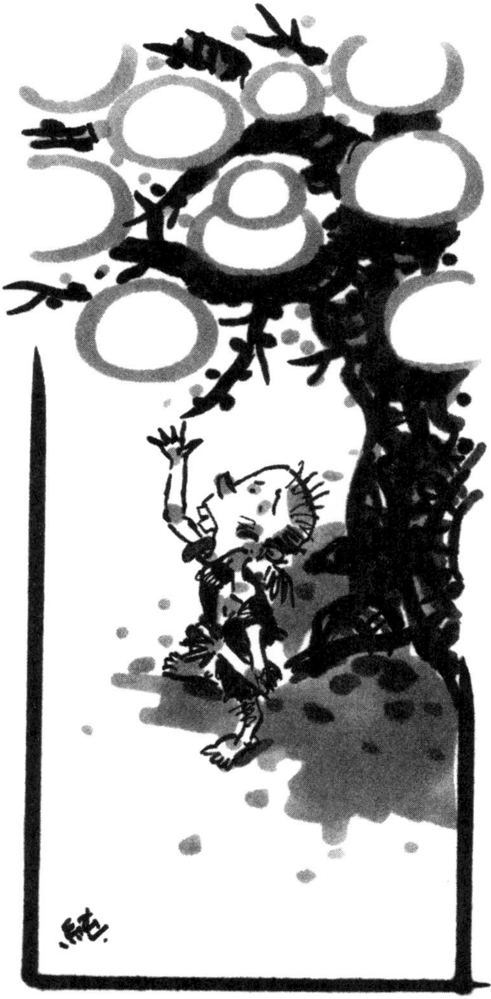
純

57

Shippai wa seikō no haha.

Failure is the mother of success.

失敗は、成功の母

58

Gei wa mi no ada.

One's art may be one's enemy.

芸は身の仇

59

Noren ni ude-ōshi

Strong-arming a shop curtain.

暖簾に腕押し

60

Kerai to naraneba kerai wa tsukaenu.

Unless you have been a servant,
you cannot use a servant.

家来と成らねば家来は使えぬ

61

Tanoshimi ni onna nashi otoko nashi.

In the pursuit of pleasure, there is no difference between a woman and a man.

楽しみ〜女なし男かなし

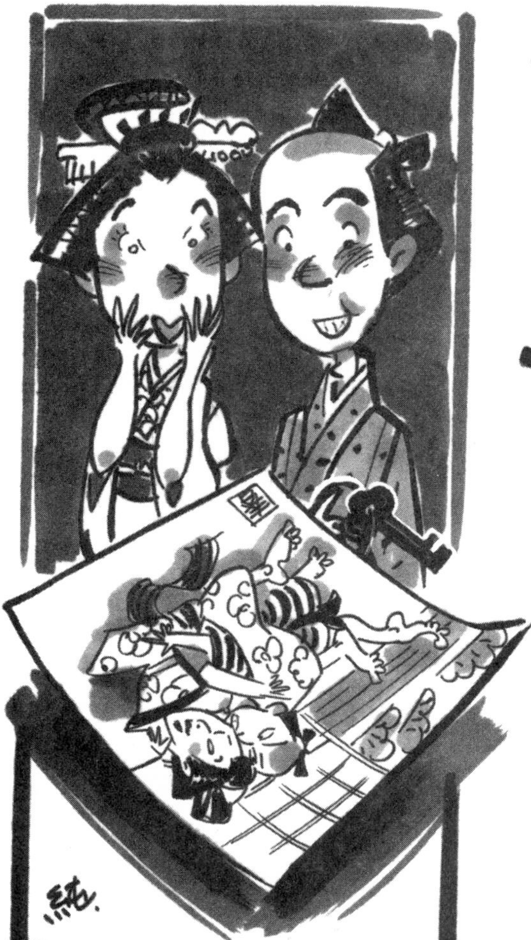

62

Namari wa tō to nasu-bekarazu.

Lead should not be made into a sword.

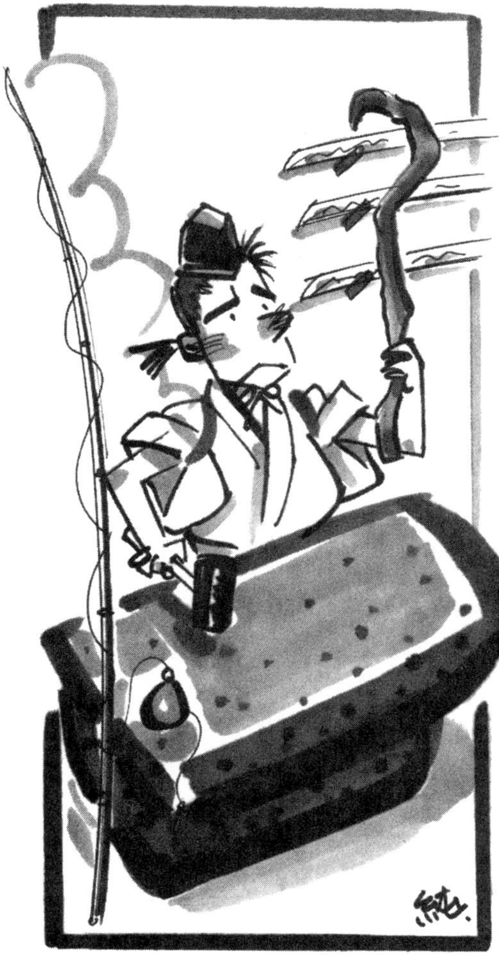
純.

鉛は刀となすべからず

63

Tori wa furusu ni kaeru.

Birds return to old nests.

鳥は古巣に帰る

64

Kokoro futatsu ni, mi wa hitotsu.

One body for two hearts.

心は二つ身は一つ

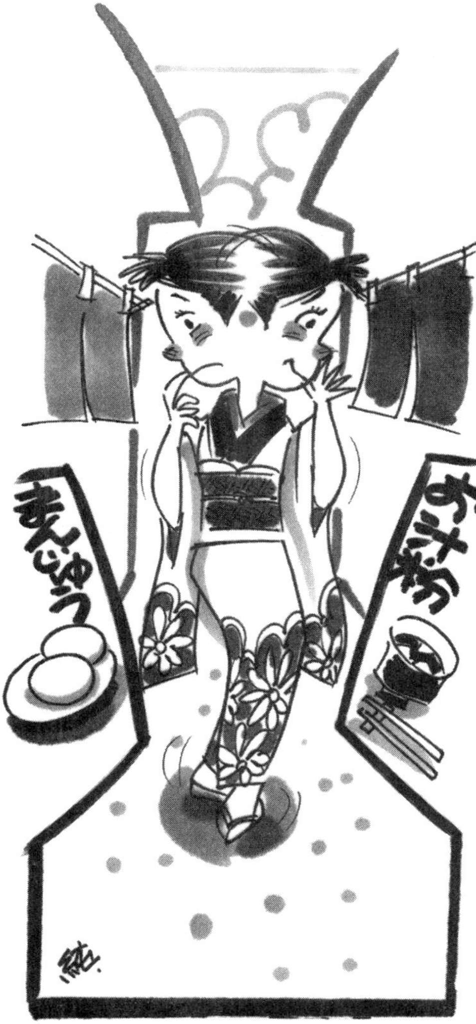
まんじゅう
お汁粉

65

Ware-nabe ni toji-buta.

A repaired lid on a broken pot.

破れ鍋に綴じ蓋

66

Fumi wa yaritashi kaku-te wa motazu.

I want to write but have no writing hand.

文はやりたし書く手は持たず

春

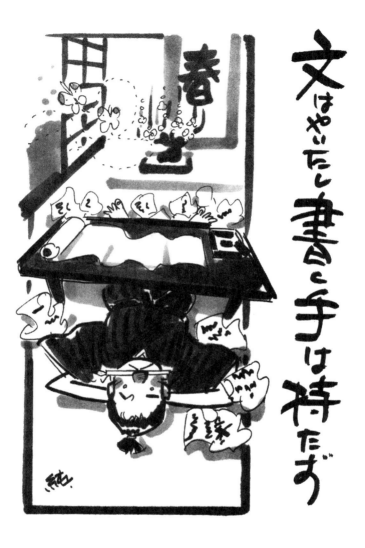

67

Waranbe ni hana motaseru gotoshi.

Like giving flowers to a child.

童べに花持たせるごとし

68

Ichiyō ochite tenka no aki o shiru.

One leaf falls, and you know that autumn
is in the land.

一葉落ちて天下の秋を知る

69

Iki no ka no kusaki wa nushi shirazu.

The possessor of bad breath does not notice the odor.

息の香の臭きは主知らず

70

Jōchi to kagu to wa utsurazu.

Wise men and fools do not change.

上知と下愚とは移らず

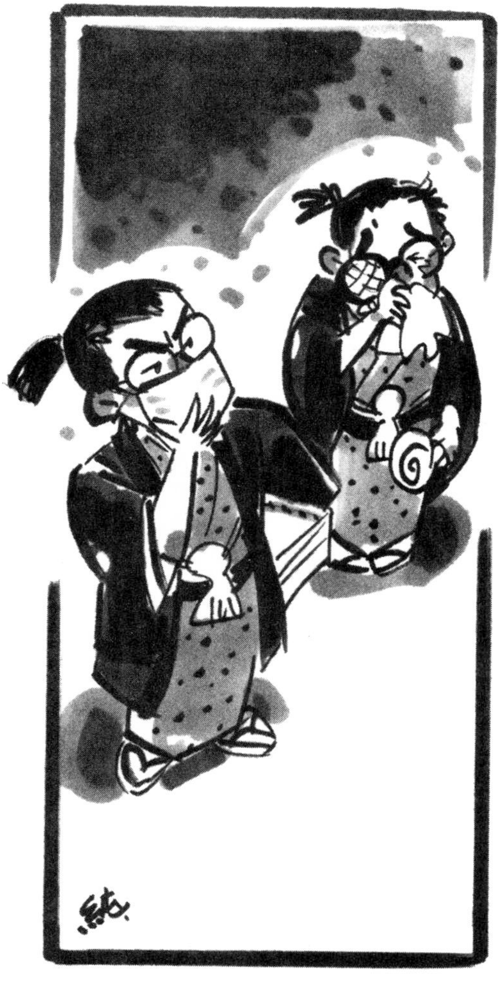

71

Sode kara kaji.

A fire from a kimono sleeve.

袖から火事

72

Yamai o mamorite i o imu.

Shun the doctor to protect one's disease.

病を護りて医を忌む

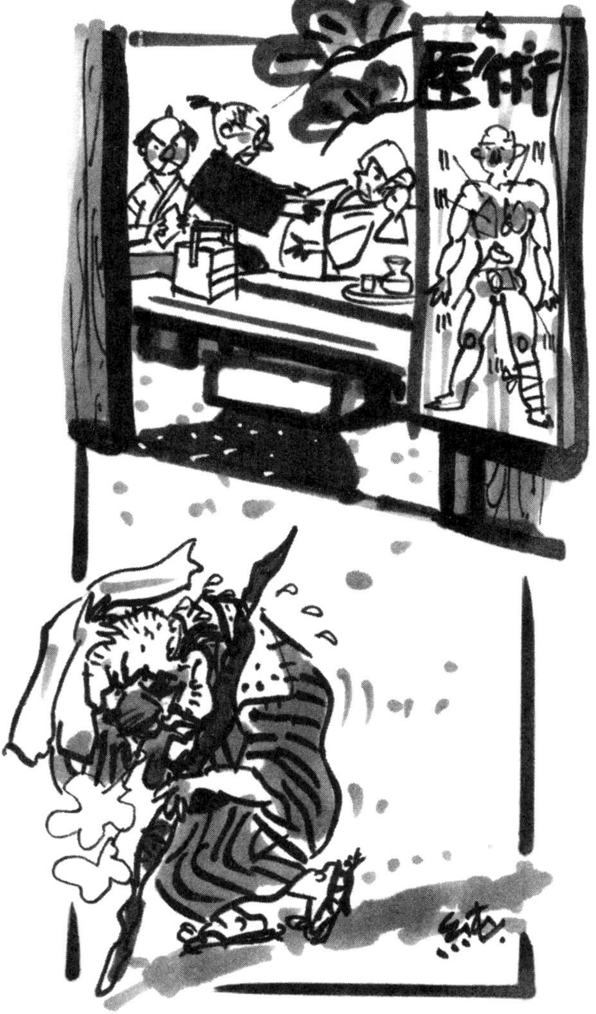
医術

73

Abata mo ekubo.

Even pockmarks may look like dimples.

痘痕と靨

74

Atsui koi wa same-yasui.

Hot love cools easily.

熱い恋は冷めやすい

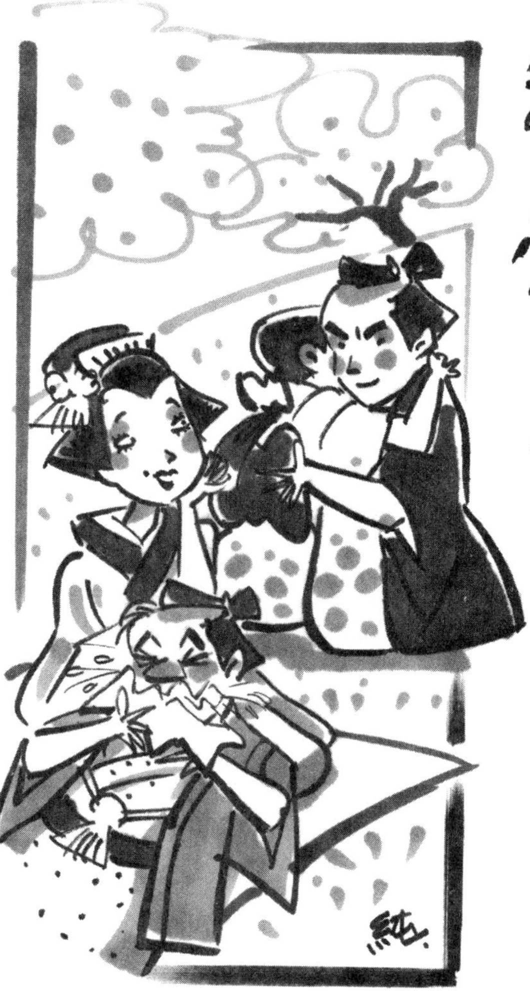
純

75

Hyōtan de namazu o osaeru.

To pin down a catfish with a gourd.

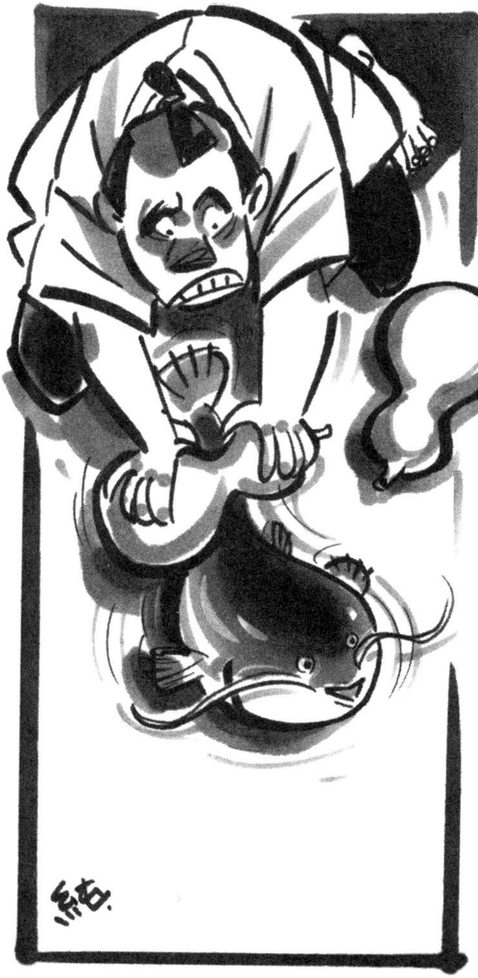

瓢箪で鯰を押さえる

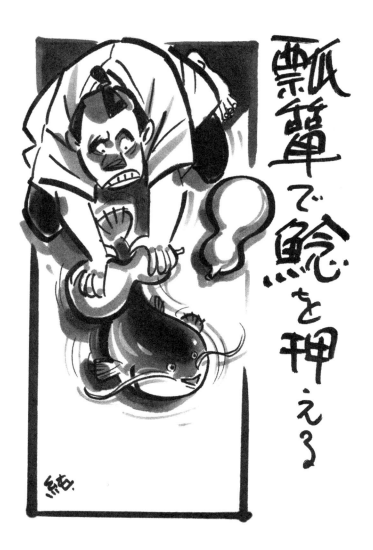

76

Minasoko no hari o sagasu.

To search for a needle at the bottom of
the water.

水底の針を捜す

77

Setchin de yari o tsukau yō.

Like wielding a spear in a toilet.

雪隠で槍を使うよう

78

En wa i na mono.

Marriage is a curious thing.

縁は異なもの

79

Hyakusen hyakushō wa zen no zen naru mono ni arazu.

A hundred victories in a hundred battles is good, but the virtuous man does otherwise.

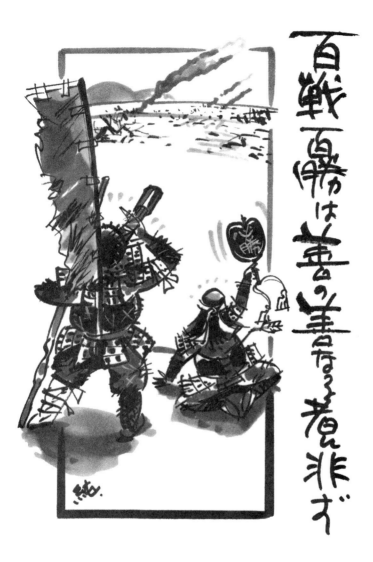

百戦百勝は善の善なる者に非ず

80

Hadaka de mono o otosu tameshi nashi.

There are no instances of a naked person dropping things.

裸で恥を落とす例なし

81

Yokoguruma o osu.

To push a cart sideways.

横車を押す

82

Suki-koso mono no jōzu nare.

One becomes skilled at the very thing one likes.

好きこそ物の上手なれ

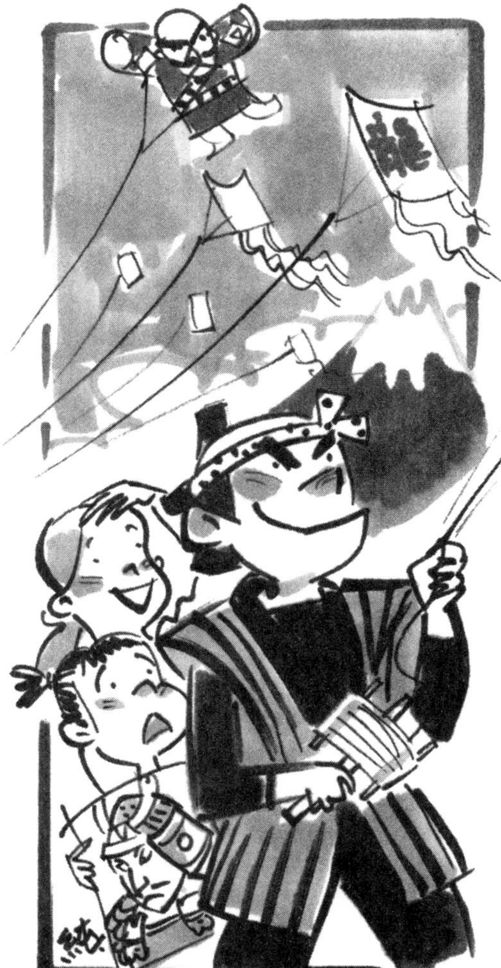
龍

83

Tonari no hana wa akai.

The neighbor's flowers are red.

隣りの花は赤い

84

Sui wa mi o kuu.

Fashion eats up the body.

粋は身を食う

85

Tera no tonari ni mo oni ga sumu.

Devils, too, live alongside the temple.

寺の隣りに鬼が住む

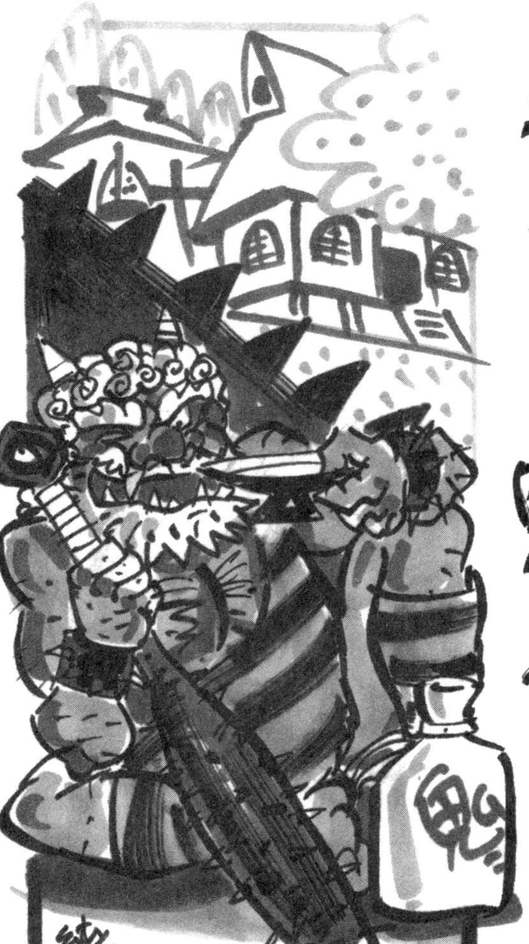
鬼
純.

86

Jibun no atama no hae o oe.

Brush the flies away from your own head.

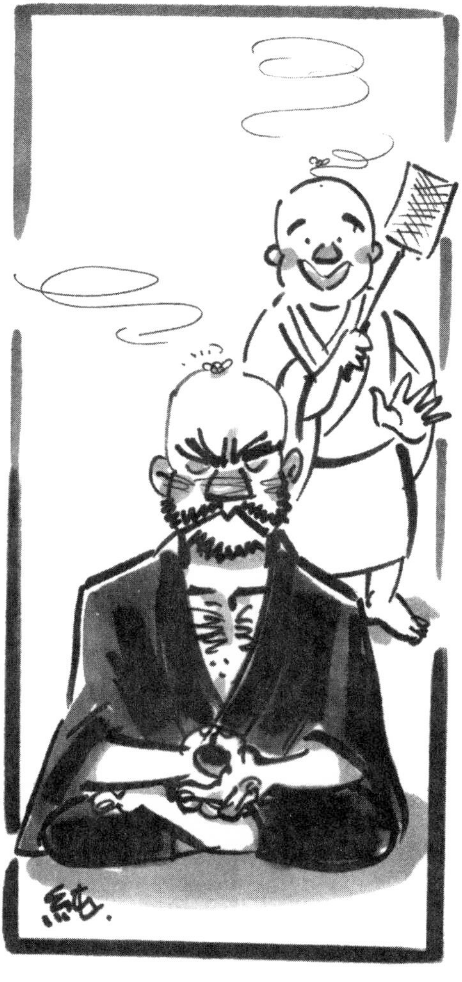

自分の頭の蠅を追え

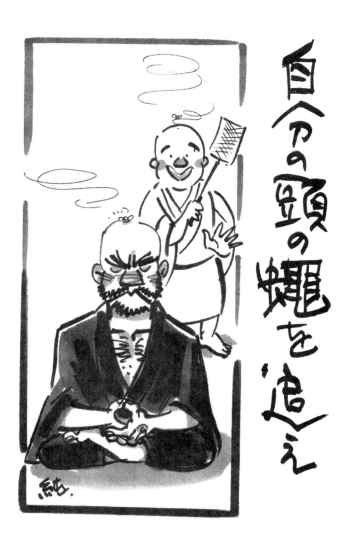

87

Bō hodo negatte hari hodo kanau.

Ask for as much as a pole and be given only a needle.

棒ほど願って針ほど叶う

88

Hisashi o kashite omoya o torareru.

Lend the eaves and the main building
will be taken.

庇を貸して母屋を取られる

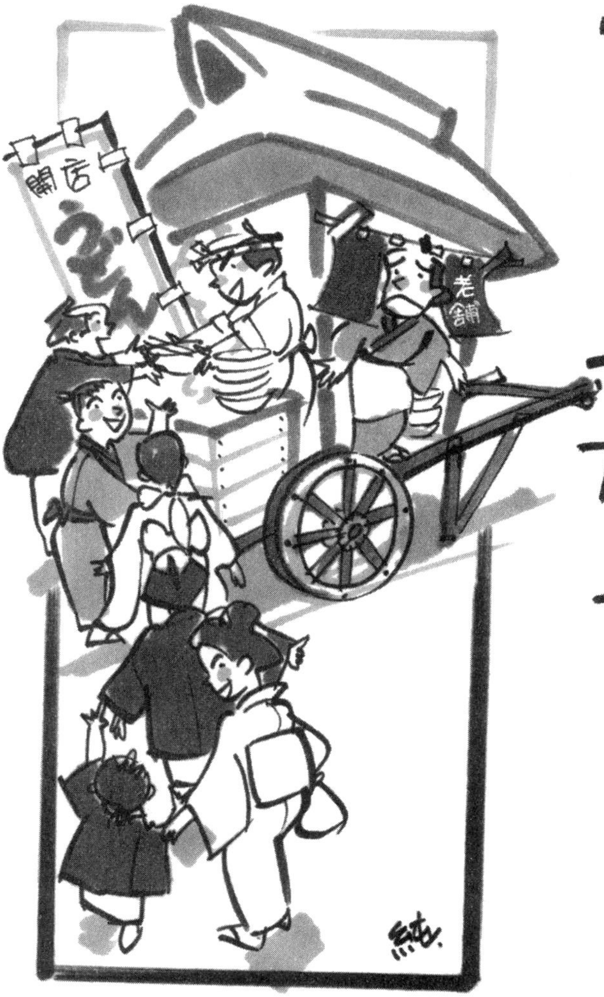
開店
うどん
老舗

89

Idobata no chawan.

A teacup on the edge of a well.

井戸端の茶碗

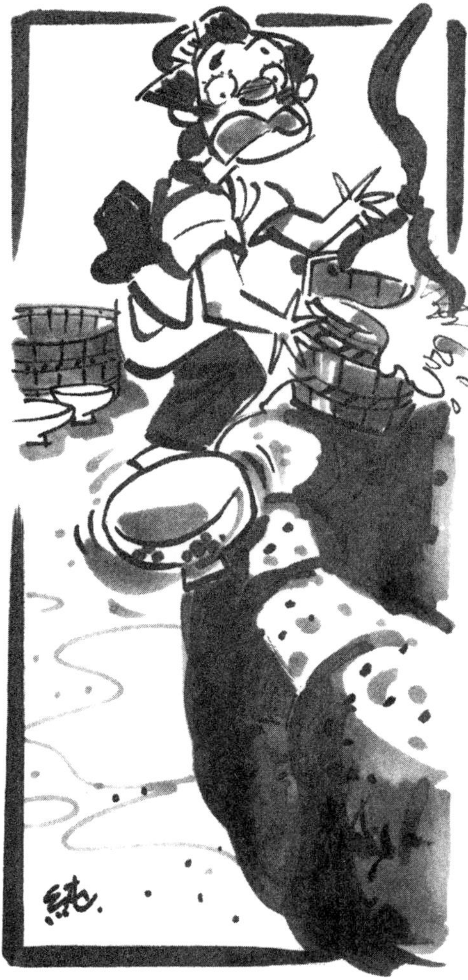
純.

90

Shirazaru wa ayamareru ni masaru.

Better not to know than to be wrong.

知らざるは　誤れるに勝る

91

Suso totte kata e tsugu.

Taking from the hem to patch the shoulder.

裾取って肩へ継ぐ

92

Iwashi no kashira mo shinjin kara.

Put faith even in a sardine head.

鰯の頭も信心から

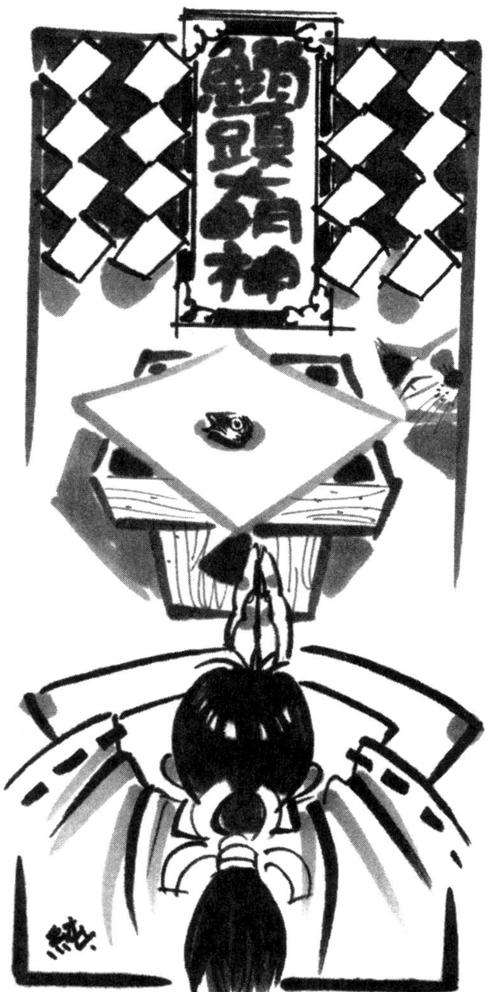
鰯頭大明神

93

Hebi ni kamarete kuchi-nawa ni ojiru.

A person bitten by a snake will fear a rotted rope.

蛇に噛まれて朽ち縄に怖じる

94

Kane ga kane o yobu.

Money attracts money.

金が金を呼ぶ

95

Amadare ishi o ugatsu.

Raindrops will wear through a stone.

雨垂れ石を穿つ

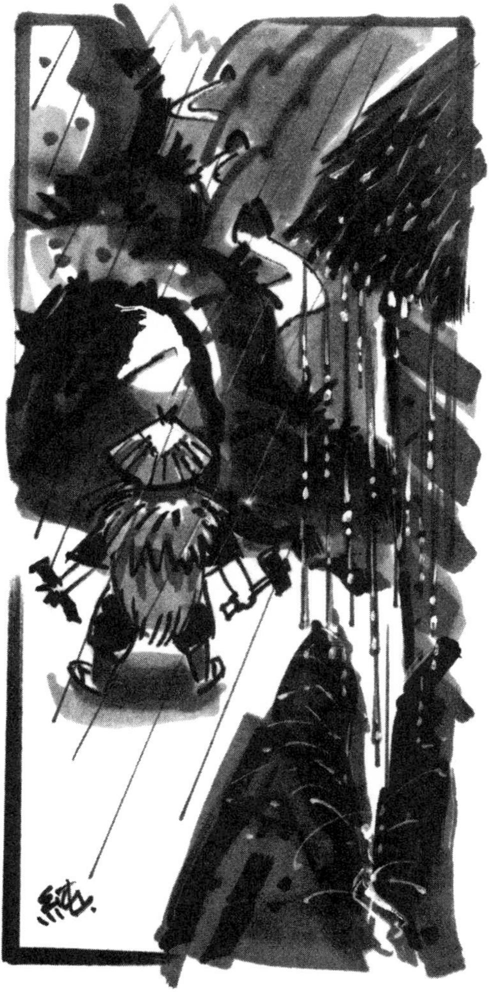

96

Deichū no hasu.

A lotus flower in the mire.

泥中の蓮

97

Mitai ga yamai.

Wanting to see is a weakness.

見たが疲

98

Tō messen to shite hi o masu.

A candle flares up just before extinguishing.

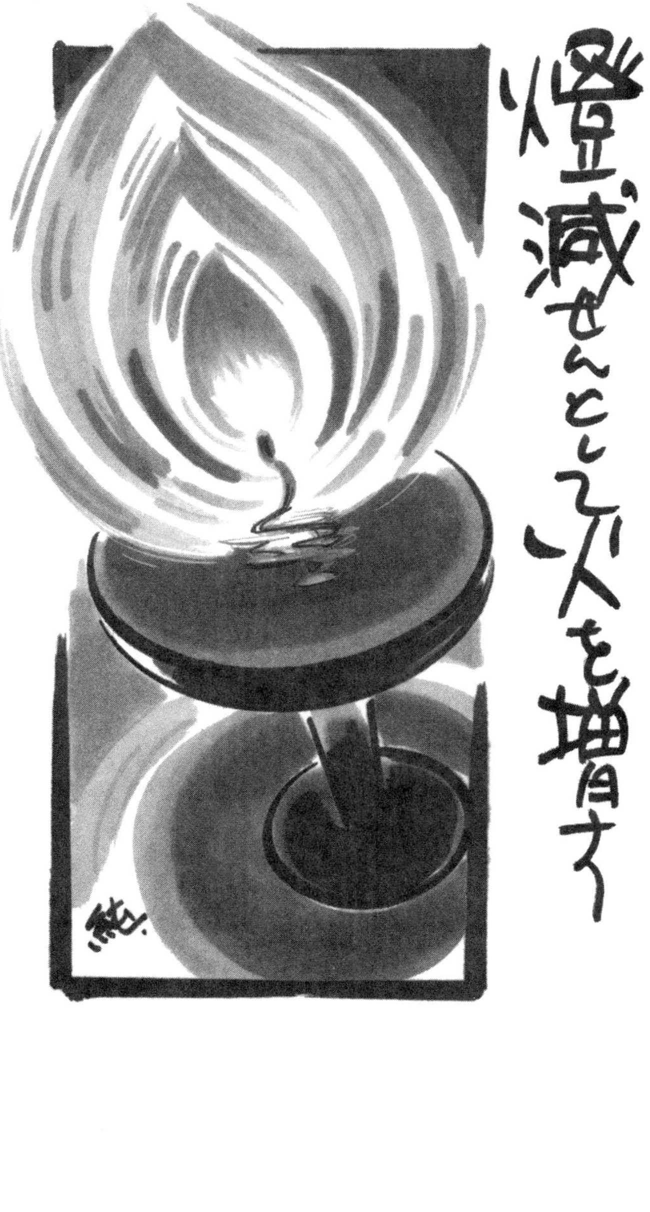
燈滅せんとして光を増す

99

Nakute nana kuse.

Nothing if not seven habits.

無くて七癖

100

Oreru yori nabike.

Better to bow than to break.

折れるより靡け

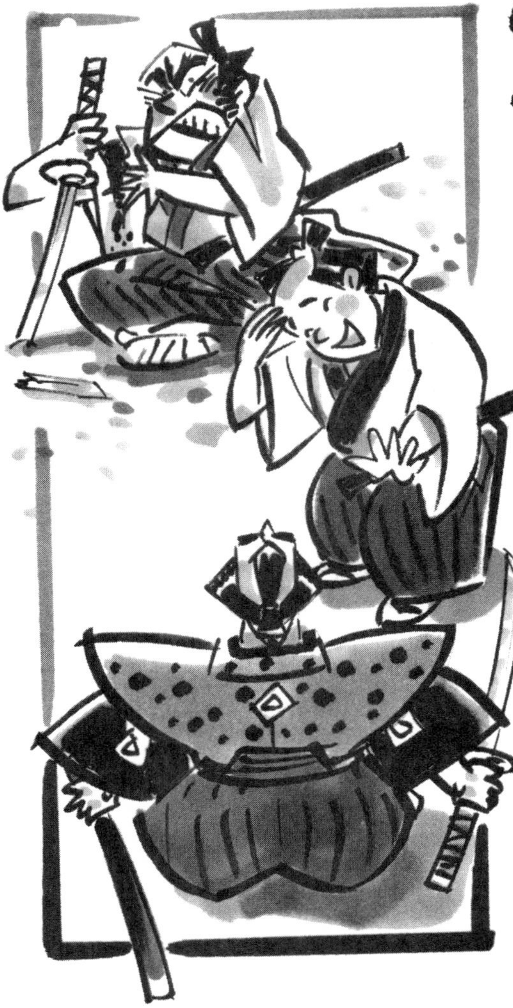

List of Proverbs
with English Equivalents

1 **石仏も物を言う**
Ishibotoke mo mono o iu.
Every picture tells a story.

2 **獅子身中の虫**
Shishi shinchuu no mushi.
Nourishing a snake in one's bosom.

3 **手者より無者が怖い**
Tesha yori nasha ga kowai.
Fear the man who has nothing left to lose.

4 **月雪花は一度に眺められぬ**
Tsuki yuki hana wa ichido ni nagamerarenu.
To every thing there is a season.

5 **長口上は欠伸の種**
Nagakoujou wa akubi no tane.
Brevity is the soul of wit.

6 **無用の用**
Muyou no you.
All is grist for the mill.

7 **身代につるる心**
Shindai ni tsururu-kokoro.
Money makes the world go round.

8 **死んだ子の年を数える**
Shindako no toshi o kazoeru.
A fruitless endeavor.

9　猫に小判

Neko ni koban.

Pearls before swine.

10　礼も過ぎれば無礼になる

Rei mo sugireba burei ni naru.

Killing with kindness.

11　大海は芥を択ばず

Taikai wa akuta o erabazu.

A generous soul accepts everyone.

12　大器晩成

Taiki bansei.

Last, but not least.

13　善き分別は雪隠で出る

Yoki funbetsu wa setchin de deru.

Inspiration strikes in the unlikeliest of places.

14　寝耳に水

Nemimi ni mizu.

A shock to the system.

15　死に馬に針をさす

Shini uma ni hari o sasu.

Like flogging a dead horse.

16　へそで茶を沸かす

Heso de cha o wakasu.

A belly laugh.

17　憎まれっ子世にはばかる

Nikkumarekko yo ni habakaru.

Evil men flourish like the green bay tree.

18 瑠璃もは璃も照らせば光る

Ruri mo hari mo teraseba hikaru.

Encouragement brings out the best in people.

19 喉元過ぎれば熱さを忘れる

Nodomoto sugireba atsusa o wasureru.

Out of sight, out of mind.

20 聞いて極楽見て地獄

Kiite gokuraku mite jigoku.

Seeing is believing.

21 楽は苦の種、苦は楽の種

Raku wa ku no tane, ku wa raku no tane.

You have to take the rough with the smooth.

22 転ばぬ先の杖

Korobanu saki no tsue.

Better safe than sorry.

23 ただより高いものはない

Tada yori takai mono wa nai.

There's no such thing as a free lunch.

24 畳の上の水練

Tatami no ue no suiren.

Knowledge alone will get you only so far.

25 四角な座敷を丸く掃く

Shikaku na zashiki o maruku haku.

To cut corners.

26 職がたき

Shoku gataki.

Two of a trade don't get along.

27 目は口程に物を言う

Me wa kuchi hodo ni mono o iu.

The eyes are the windows of the soul.

28 盗人と智者の相は同じ

Nusubito to chisha no sou wa onaji.

You can't judge a book by its cover.

29 月夜に米の飯

Tsuki-yo ni kome no meshi.

The simple things in life.

30 水魚の交わり

Suigyo no majiwari.

As a fish takes to water.

31 こう龍悔い有り

Kouryou kui ari.

The bigger they are, the harder they fall.

32 盗み食いはうまい

Nusumi-gui wa umai.

Stolen cherries are sweeter.

33 まな板の鯉

Manaita no koi.

A calf led to the slaughter.

34 砂を噛む

Suna o kamu.

To chew the carpet.

35 情けに刃向かう刃なし

Nasake ni hamukau yaiba nashi.

You catch more flies with honey than vinegar.

36 一条の矢は折べく十条は折べからず

Ichijou no ya wa orubeku,

Juujou wa orubekarazu.

There is strength in numbers.

37 話し上手の聞き下手

Hanashi-jouzu no kiki-beta

None so deaf as those who will not hear.

38 ぼろを着ても心は錦

Boro o kite mo kokoro wa nishiki.

Beneath that rough exterior beats a heart of gold.

39 善なるもの必ず美ならず

Zen naru mono kanarazu bi narazu.

Beauty is only skin deep.

40 鵜の真似をする烏水に溺れる

U no mane o suru karasu, mizu ni oboreru.

To thine own self be true.

41 早く熟すれば早く腐る

Hayaku jukusureba hayaku kusaru.

Easy come, easy go.

42 盲蛇に怖じず

Mekura hebi ni ojizu.

Ignorance is bliss.

43 学問に近道なし

Gakumon ni chikamichi nashi.

There is no royal road to learning.

44 敵に塩を贈る

Teki ni shio o okuru.

Return good for evil.

4 5　有る一文無い千両

Aru ichi mon nai sen ryou.

A bird in the hand is worth two in the bush.

4 6　碁に勝って勝負に負ける

Go ni katte shoubu ni makeru.

It's not whether you win or lose, but how you play the game.

4 7　着れば着寒し

Kireba kizamushi.

The greedy are never satisfied.

4 8　士族の商法

Shizoku no shouhou.

A fish out of water.

4 9　燈台下暗し

Toudai moto kurashi.

Sometimes you can't see the forest for the trees.

5 0　えん豆は日陰でもはじける

Endou wa hikage de mo hajikeru.

Some thrive on adversity.

5 1　河豚は食いたし命は惜しし

Fugu wa kuitashi inochi wa oshishi.

He who plays with fire gets burnt.

5 2　敗軍の将は兵を語らず

Haigun no shou wa hei o katarazu.

People in glass houses shouldn't throw stones.

53 隠すことは口より出すな

Kakusu koto wa kuchi yori dasuna.

Loose lips sink ships.

54 居は気を移す

Kyo wa ki o utsusu.

You are what you eat.

55 昔は今の鏡

Mukashi wa ima no kagami.

History goes in cycles.

56 木に餅がなる

Ki ni mochi ga naru.

Money doesn't grow on trees.

57 失敗は成功の母

Shippai wa seikou no haha.

Learn from experience.

58 芸は身の仇

Gei wa mi no ada.

Don't get carried away.

59 のれんに腕押し

Noren ni ude-oshi.

Like boxing with a shadow.

60 家来と成らねば家来は使えぬ

Kerai to naraneba kerai wa tsukaenu.

It takes one to know one.

61 楽しみに女なし男なし

Tanoshimi ni onna nashi otoko nashi.

What's sauce for the goose is sauce for the gander.

62 鉛は刀となすべからず

Namari wa tou to nasu-bekarazu.

You can't make a silk purse from a sow's ear.

63 鳥は古巣に帰る

Tori wa furusu ni kaeru.

There's no place like home.

64 心は二つ身は一つ

Kokoro wa futatsu, mi wa hitotsu.

To be of two minds.

65 破鍋に綴じ蓋

Ware-nabe ni toji-buta.

Two of a kind.

66 文はやりたし書く手は持たず

Fumi wa yaritashi kaku-te wa motazu.

Pen in hand, heart in mouth.

67 童べに花持たせるごとし

Waranbe ni hana motaseru gotoshi.

A bull in a china shop.

68 一葉落ちて天下の秋を知る

Ichiyou ochite tenka no aki o shiru.

A robin is a harbinger of spring.

69 息の香の臭きは主知らず

Iki no ka no kusaki wa nushi shirazu.

Before complaining of the mote in your brother's
eye, first remove the beam from your own.

70 上知と下愚とは移らず

Jouchi to kagu to wa utsurazu.

The pure of heart stay pure.

7 1　袖から火事

Sode kara kaji.

For want of a nail, a kingdom was lost.

7 2　病を護りて医を忌む

Yamai o mamorite i o imu.

Hide your shame.

7 3　痘痕もえくぼ

Abata mo ekubo.

Love is blind.

7 4　熱い恋は冷めやすい

Atsui koi wa same-yasui.

The hotter the flame, the quicker it dies.

7 5　瓢箪で鯰を押える

Hyoutan de namazu o osaeru.

Slippery as an eel.

7 6　水底の針を捜す

Minasoko no hari o sagasu.

To look for a needle in a haystack.

7 7　雪隠で槍を使うよう

Setchin de yari o tsukau you.

No room to swing a cat.

7 8　縁は異なもの

En wa i na mono.

Fate has a hand in weddings.

7 9　百戦百勝は善の善なる者に非ず

Hyakusen hyakushou wa zen no zen naru

mono ni arazu.

The best defense is avoidance.

8 0   裸で物を落とす例なし

Hadaka de mono o otosu tameshi nashi.

Nothing left to hide.

8 1   横車を押す

Yokoguruma o osu.

To push a rock up a mountain.

8 2   好きこそ物の上手なれ

Suki-koso mono no jouzu nare.

Do what you love, and success will follow.

8 3   隣の花は赤い

Tonari no hana wa akai.

The grass is greener on the other side of the fence.

8 4   粋は身を食う

Sui wa mi o kuu.

You must suffer to be beautiful.

8 5   寺の隣にも鬼が住む

Tera no tonari ni mo oni ga sumu.

Evil and good live side by side.

8 6   自分の頭の蝿を追え

Jibun no atama no hae o oe.

Mind your own business.

8 7   棒ほど願って針ほど叶う

Bou hodo negatte hari hodo kanau.

You can't always get what you want.

8 8   庇を貸して母屋を取られる

Hisashi o kashite omoya o torareru.
Give them an inch and they'll take a mile.

8 9　井戸端の茶碗

Idobata no chawan.
A house of cards.

9 0　知らざるは誤れるに勝る

Shirazaru wa ayamareru ni masaru.
Better to remain silent and be thought ignorant
than to open one's mouth and remove all doubt.

9 1　裾取って肩へ継ぐ

Suso totte kata e tsugu.
Robbing Peter to pay Paul.

9 2　鰯の頭も信心から

Iwashi no kashira mo shinjin kara.
Everyone has to believe in something.

9 3　蛇に噛まれて朽ち縄に怖じる

Hebi ni kamarete kuchi-nawa ni ojiru.
A burnt cat will avoid a cold stove.

9 4　金が金を呼ぶ

Kane ga kane o yobu.
The rich get richer.

9 5　雨垂れ石を穿つ

Amadare ishi o ugatsu.
Slow and steady wins the race.

9 6　泥中の蓮

Deichuu no hasu.
A diamond in the rough.

9 7　見たいが病

Mitai ga yamai.

Curiosity killed the cat.

9 8　燈滅せんとして火を増す

Tou messen to shite hi o masu.

Old coals burn brightest.

9 9　無くて七癖

Nakute nana kuse.

Everyone has a few peculiarities.

1 0 0　折れるよりなびけ

Oreru yori nabike.

Be like the willow, not like the oak.

In this List of Proverbs, non-jouyou kanji have been replaced with hiragana or modern kanji.